Copycat Recipes

Delicious Recipes from Your Favorite Restaurants

by Johanna Merkenson

Sommario

Introduction

Occasionally, you go into a restaurant's food and talk about just how it is so scrumptious that you can eat it daily. While frequenting a details dining establishment just to consume your preferred recipe is fantastic for the proprietor's organization, it can be harming to your financial resources and also really troublesome, specifically if the establishment isn't located near you.

Thankfully, I have assembled dozens of the best copycat dishes in this book to aid you recreate your preferred dining establishment meals right in the very convenience of your residence. All the featured recipes are comprehensive and easy-to-follow so you can quickly enjoy what you are presently food craving for.

Numerous households love heading out to their favorite restaurants to eat; most eat out regarding 3 times a week. If you have a large family members, or even a fairly tiny family of hefty eaters, you know that the costs quickly add up. It is enjoyable going out with your family to consume. However you don't always have to enter into the car as well as head to the dining establishment to get the favorite meals for your family members. You can surprise and also even impress your household and loved ones with a preferred dining establishment meal by doing it in your very own cooking area at home. With rates rising in all retail industries, having a much less costly option to dining in restaurants may be a smart idea. Your family members will constantly appreciate the initiative you make to obtain a wonderful dining establishment dish to serve for day-to-day meals. Dining establishment dishes have actually taken a number of years to ideal in the majority of circumstances, yet you can have them to provide to your family and friends, tried and verified.

So why not have a little enjoyable in the kitchen area by preparing the dishes you love from your favored restaurants? Simply consider all the cash you will certainly be saving by not driving over there, spending for your dishes, and tipping the steward! Dining out is costly and also can cost you $16 or more per dish than if you had actually simply eaten at house. Plus, when you prepare at home, you have complete control of what will get on your plate, as well as the flavor will certainly make you appreciate home-cooked food. Absolutely nothing contrasts to homemade food. It's fresh, it's tasty, and you can consume as long as you like, as you regulate the amounts.

If you are wondering where you can get these recipes or are concerned because you are not quite a "chef" in your cooking area, do not worry, I have you covered. This publication features thorough dishes as well as guidelines on exactly how to prepare one of the most prominent dishes from several of the most effective restaurants. You will certainly be able to locate the most effective morning meals, appetizers, treats, and also main course recipes from well-known restaurants.

So check out the adhering to dishes, and start preparing your next home-style restaurant meal while maintaining the calorie count reduced. Make these gorgeous homemade recipes without going to your favorite dining establishment.

Chapter 1: Breakfast

Starbucks' Pumpkin Cream Cheese Muffins

Full of autumn flavors and spices, filled with cream cheese, and sprinkled with crunchy candied pumpkin seeds. You'll be happy to be making your own at home!

Preparation Time: 10 minutes

Cooking time: 65 minutes

Servings: 8

Ingredients:

Cream Cheese Filling

1 (8-ounce) package cream cheese, cubed, at room temperature

½ cup sugar

1 teaspoon vanilla

Candied Pumpkin Seeds

3 tablespoons sugar

½ cup pumpkin seeds

¼ teaspoon cinnamon

Muffin Batter:

1 cup pumpkin puree

⅓ cup vegetable oil

½ cup sugar

½ cup brown sugar

2 eggs

1 teaspoon baking soda

¼ teaspoon salt

1½ teaspoons cinnamon

1 teaspoon ground ginger

½ teaspoon ground cloves

½ teaspoon ground allspice

2 cups flour, divided

¼ cup milk

Directions:

Prepare the filling first. Beat the ingredients together until smooth. Place in refrigerator to make firm.

Prepare the candied pumpkin seeds. Line a cookie sheet with parchment paper. Place sugar in saucepan over medium heat. When sugar begins to boil and brown, reduce heat to low. Stir in seeds and cinnamon. Keep stirring until sugar is caramelized and sticky, causing the seeds to form clusters. Transfer seeds to parchment paper to cool. When cooled, break clusters into individual seeds.

Preheat oven to 350°F and line muffin tins.

Beat together pumpkin puree, oil and sugars, just to combine.

Beat in eggs, baking soda, salt, spices, and 1 cup flour.

Lastly, beat in milk and remaining flour. Mix just to incorporate. Do not over-mix.

Fill each muffin cup or tin up to about ¾ full.

Place a tablespoonful of cream cheese filling on top of each.

Sprinkle with candied pumpkin seeds.

Bake until a toothpick inserted in one or two of the muffins comes out clean (about 15 minutes).

Let cool on a wire rack before removing from muffin pan.

Cinnabon's Monkey Bread

Yummy cinnamon rolls, joined together with a "glue" of syrup and honey, and drizzled with white frosting.

Preparation Time: 10 minutes

Cooking time: 45 minutes

Servings: 8

Ingredients

3 cans Cinnabon cinnamon roll dough

1 cup sugar

1 tablespoon cinnamon

½ cup (1 stick) butter, melted

½ cup brown sugar

2 tablespoons honey

Frosting (optional)

1 tablespoon milk

1 teaspoon butter

2 cups powdered sugar

Directions:

Preheat oven to 400°F. Grease a Bundt or loaf pan.

Cut each dough roll into half and roll into balls.

Combine sugar and cinnamon and place in a plastic bag or shallow dish.

Coat the dough with the cinnamon sugar.

Fit the dough into the pan.

In a bowl, stir the butter, brown sugar and honey together until all the sugar is dissolved.

Pour the honey mixture evenly over the dough in the pan.

Bake until fragrant and browned, or with internal temperature of 190–200°F (about 20 minutes).

If using frosting, prepare it while the bread is baking. Place ingredients in a saucepan over low heat; stirring continuously until smooth. It should be a good consistency for drizzling. Add a few drops of water or milk if too thick.

Let the bread cool down for about 5 minutes before removing from the pan. Drizzle with frosting (optional).

Denny's Pancake Puppies

If you like fresh donut holes, you'll probably like these little bite-sized balls of pancake wrapped in powdered sugar. Serve with a small bowl of dipping syrup.

Preparation Time: 10 minutes

Cooking time: 50 minutes

Servings: 8

Ingredients:

Vegetable oil, for frying

1/3 cup milk

1 cup Aunt Jemima Original Pancake Mix

1 egg

1 tablespoon finely chopped white chocolate chips

½ cup chopped dried blueberries

Powdered sugar, for dusting

Directions:

1. In a deep fryer, Preheat oil.

2. Combine pancake mixture, milk, and egg into a medium dish.

3. Add the chocolate chips and blueberries and stir.

4. Let the batter sit in to thicken for 10 minutes.

5. Use an oil-coated ice cream scoop to make a batter ball, when the oil is hot, and drop it into the hot oil.

6. Cook for 2½–3 minutes, until the batter is dark brown.

7. Place on paper towels to drain and top with powdered sugar.

IHOP Chicken Fajita Omelette

These days you'll see fajitas everywhere you look at the menu. There are fajita omelettes, fajita nachos, and now fajita burritos. This is a perfect recipe for using leftover fajita fixings.

Preparation Time: 10 minutes
Cooking time: 40 minutes
Servings: 8

Ingredients:

¼ cup salsa

2 eggs

½ cup leftover fajitas (chicken, onions, and peppers)

1 teaspoon water

½ cup Mexican cheese, shredded

Directions:

1. Beat together the eggs and water in a small bowl.

2. Pour the egg mixture into a medium skillet and cook for 1–2 minutes over medium heat until the egg starts to set.

3. Mix in the chicken, peppers, and onions.

4. Fold the omelet half way round. Turn off fire.

5. Top with Salsa and Cheese.

6. Close the skillet with a cover and let it sit until the cheese has melted.

Corn Muffins

Preparation Time: 15 minutes
Cooking Time: 30 minutes

Serving: 4

Ingredients:

Four tablespoons sugar

Four tablespoons butter

Four tablespoons liquid non-dairy creamer

Four tablespoons yellow cornmeal

3/4 cup self-rising flour

Directions:

Firstly, add ingredients to the bowl and beat well until it looks like a smooth cake batter.

Divide the batter into eight greased cupcake wells and fill the remaining 4 with water.

After that you have to bake for 16 to 18 minutes at 400 ° F, or till tester is inserted into the centers. Put the pan aside to cool for a few minutes, then remove with two forks so that the water is not disturbed.

Chapter 2: Appetizers

World Famous Chicken Crunch

It's such a crunchy and delicious dish! You will love it once you try it!

Preparation Time: 10 minutes

Cooking Time: 10 minutes

Servings: 4

Ingredients:

1-pound chicken tenders

1 cup Cap'n Crunch cereal

2 teaspoon ground black pepper

1 cup milk

1 cup flour

2 organic eggs, large

1 tablespoon granulated onion

1 cup corn flakes

Vegetable oil for frying

1 tablespoon granulated garlic

Directions:

Pulse the cereals in a blender until you get fine crumbs like consistency and then pour into a large bowl. Combine flour together with garlic, onion & pepper in separate bowl.

Beat the eggs & combine them with milk in a separate bowl. Dredge the breast tenders, first into the milk mixture and then into the flour mixture & lastly into the cereal crumbs.

Deep fry until cooked thoroughly, for 3 to 4 minutes, at 325 F. Serve with some Creole mustard on side and enjoy.

Copycat Mozzarella Sticks from TGI Fridays

This is a great recipe for anyone who loves mozzarella sticks.

Preparation Time: 5 minutes

Cooking Time: 5 minutes

Servings: 6

Ingredients:

⅔ cup all-purpose flour

2 large eggs

¼ cup milk

1 cup Japanese breadcrumbs

½ cup Parmesan cheese, shredded

1 tablespoon dried parsley

½ teaspoon garlic salt

½ teaspoon seasoning salt

8 pieces mozzarella string cheese

1-quart vegetable oil

Marinara sauce

Directions:

Add flour to a bowl. Then, in a separate bowl, mix eggs and milk. Add breadcrumbs, Parmesan, parsley, garlic salt, and seasoning salt in a third bowl and mix well.

Line baking sheet with wax paper. Set aside.

Cut mozzarella pieces in half vertically so that you will end up with 16 mozzarella sticks. Then, for each piece, dredge first in flour, followed by egg wash, and third in breadcrumb mixture. Dredge again in egg wash and breadcrumbs for a thicker coat. Place pieces on prepared baking sheet and place in freezer for at least 1 hour or overnight.

To prepare mozzarella sticks preheat deep fryer to 350°F.

About 4 sticks at a time, deep fry for about 30 seconds or until golden brown. Using a slotted spoon, transfer to a rack or plate lined with paper towels to drain.

Serve warm with marinara sauce.

Queso Blanco Dip

Are you in the mood for a Mexican dish? Then you should try this one as soon as possible!

Preparation time: 5 minutes
Cooking time 10 minutes

Servings: 10

Ingredients:

1 tablespoon vegetable oil

2 tablespoons jalapeño pepper, finely minced

⅓ cup white onion, finely chopped

4 cups white cheddar cheese, shredded

2 cups Monterey Jack cheese, shredded

½ cup half and half

½ cup chopped tomato

2 tablespoons cilantro, chopped

Salt and pepper to taste

Tortilla chips, for serving

Directions:

In a medium skillet, combine the vegetable oil, 1 ½ tablespoons chopped jalapeño pepper, and white onion. Sauté over medium heat until the onion is soft.

Add the cheese and half and half.

Reduce the heat to low and stir until the cheese melts, then add the fresh tomatoes and cilantro. Season to taste with salt and pepper and mix well.

Transfer the dip to a heatproof serving bowl, and garnish with the remaining jalapeño.

Serve with tortilla chips.

Red Robin Campfire Sauce

Take a look at this recipe, get all the ingredients and make it for your loved one's tonight!

Preparation Time: 10 minutes

Cooking Time: 10 minutes

Servings: 6

Ingredients:

½ cup mayo

1/8 teaspoon cayenne pepper

½ teaspoon paprika

1/8 teaspoon garlic powder

½ cup your favorite BBQ sauce

Directions:

Whisk the entire ingredients together until completely smooth; serve immediately & enjoy.

Ruby Tuesday Queso Dip

A delicious dip that will quickly become a favorite.

Preparation Time: 10 minutes

Cooking Time: 10 minutes

Servings: 6

Ingredients:

1 box chopped spinach, frozen, thawed & squeeze out any excess water (approximately 10 oz)

1 jar of Taco Bell salsa & queso (approximately 14 oz)

Directions:

Mix the entire ingredients together in a microwave-safe bowl. Heat in 1-minute intervals on high-power, stirring frequently. Continue to heat in the microwave until heated through. Serve with your favorite tortilla chips and enjoy.

Houston's Chicago Style Spinach Dip

It's a dip that will provide you enough energy to face a busy day at work. Just try it!

Preparation Time: 5 minutes

Cooking Time: 15 minutes

Servings: 10

Ingredients:

⅓ cup sour cream

2 bags of fresh Spinach (1 pound each)

⅔ cup fresh parmesan cheese, grated

1 can Artichoke Hearts, coarsely diced

1/8 pound butter

2 tablespoons onions, minced

½ cup Monterrey Jack Cheese, grated

1 teaspoon fresh garlic, minced

½ teaspoon Tabasco sauce or to taste

1 pint heavy whipping cream

¼ cup flour

2 teaspoons lemon juice, freshly squeezed

½ teaspoon salt

Directions:

Steam the spinach; strain & using a cheese cloth; squeeze the water out. Finely chop & set aside until ready to use.

Now, over moderate heat in a heavy saucepan; heat the butter until completely melted.

Add in the onions and garlic; sauté for 3 to 5 minutes.

Make a roux by adding the flour. Give everything a good stir & cook for a minute.

Slowly add in the heavy cream, stirring with a whisk to prevent lumping. The mixture would thicken at the boiling point.

When done, immediately add in the Tabasco, lemon juice, Parmesan cheese and salt.

Immediately remove the pan from heat & let stand at room temperature for 5 minutes and then stir in the sour cream.

Fold in the diced artichoke hearts, Jack cheese and dry & chopped spinach. Stir well until the cheese is completely melted.

Serve immediately and enjoy.

Loaded Boneless Wings

These Loaded Boneless Wings are not only very tasty!

Preparation   Time: 30   minutes
Cooking   Time: 50   minutes
Servings: 10

Ingredients for Veggie Queso Dip:

1 jalapeno pepper, finely chopped

½ yellow bell pepper, finely chopped

¼ teaspoon ground cumin

1 package American cheese, shredded (6 ounce)

½ red bell pepper, finely chopped

2 slices of Fontana cheese, shredded

½ teaspoon red pepper flakes

1 ball mozzarella cheese, shredded (4 ounce)

½ teaspoon olive oil

1/8 teaspoon each of garlic powder, ground black pepper, onion powder, ground nutmeg & salt

½ cup half-and-half

For Wings:

4 strips of bacon or to taste

1 package Buffalo-style boneless chicken breast halves, frozen (25.5 ounce)

½ pound cheddar cheese, shredded

3 green onions, thinly sliced

¼ pound Monterey Jack cheese, shredded

Directions:

Over medium heat in a large skillet; heat the olive oil until hot. Once done; add the yellow bell pepper together with red bell pepper & jalapeno pepper; stir well & cook for 2 to 3 minutes, until mostly tender, stirring constantly. Add the cumin; cook & stir for a minute more, until the peppers are nicely coated. Add half-&-half; let simmer until almost boiling. Decrease the heat to low and slowly stir in the mozzarella cheese, fontina cheese, American cheese, red pepper flakes, onion powder, garlic powder, nutmeg, black pepper and salt. Cook for 3 to 5 more minutes, until the cheeses are melted completely, stirring constantly.

Preheat oven to 400 F.

Place the frozen chicken breasts on a large-sized baking sheet & the bacon strips on a separate sheet.

Place both the pans in the preheated oven. Heat the chicken for 10 to 12 minutes, until thawed; remove from the oven. Continue to bake the bacon for 16 to 18 more minutes, until crispy. Leave the oven on; remove the bacon, place it on a paper towel to dry & then chop into pieces.

Place a cup of the prepared queso dip into the bottom of a large ovenproof dish or skillet. Arrange the chicken over the top & sprinkle with Monterey Jack cheese and Cheddar cheese.

Bake for 5 to 8 more minutes, until the cheeses have completely melted. Sprinkle with the chopped green onion and bacon pieces.

Five Cheese Dip

Take a look at this recipe, get all the ingredients and make it for your loved one's tonight!

Preparation Time: 5 minutes

Cooking Time: 5 minutes

Servings: 16

Ingredients:

½ cup milk

1 pkg. softened Philadelphia cream cheese (8 ounces)

¾ cup Triple cheddar cheese, finely shredded

2 tablespoon parmesan cheese, grated

Directions:

Beat the cream cheese using an electric mixer in small bowl until completely creamy.

Slowly beat in the milk until blended well.

Add in the leftover ingredients; mix well. Serve with some cut-up fresh vegetables & baked chips; enjoy.

Chapter 3: Salads and Side Dishes

Dave and Buster's Muffaletta Salad

This cold pasta salad is a variation on New Orleans big round muffaletta sandwiches that include Italian meats and cheeses. The origins of the muffaletta are from a New Orleans grocery store that was close to the farmers' market. The Italians would come in and order olive salad, lunch meats, cheese, and bread, so the store owner suggested making a sandwich out of that.

The muffaletta is being prepared with the same ingredients today and is big enough to serve a few people.

Preparation Time: 5 minutes

Cooking Time: 40 minutes

Servings: 6

Ingredients:

24 slices pepperoni

4 ounces sliced ham

2 ounces sliced salami

4 ounces sliced turkey

1 cup roasted red peppers

1 cup sliced celery

¼ cup sliced black olives

¼ cup shredded Asiago cheese

4 tablespoons chopped green onion

½ cup chopped green salad olives

3 tablespoons Italian dressing

1¼ pounds spiral pasta

1½ cups assorted lettuce

1 cup diced Roma tomatoes

¼ cup julienned spinach leaves

1 cup Italian cheese blend

Directions:

1. Cut the pepperoni, salami, ham, and turkey into thin julienne pieces. Place the meats in a large bowl.

2. Add the celery and green onions to the bowl and also the roasted peppers.

3. Chop both types of olives into the bowl and add them to the bowl.

4. Add the pasta after it has been cooked.

5. Pour the Italian dressing over the pasta and gently mix everything together.

6. Place assorted lettuce and spinach on a cold serving plate, and leave the pasta salad in the middle.

7. Place the salad mixture up in the middle of the pot.

8. Top the tomatoes and cheeses onto the salad.

Golden Corral Seafood Salad

This dish is ideal for a light and fast lunch. It can be eaten as a sandwich on top of the salad greens, in a tortilla wrap, or on bread.

Preparation Time: 5 minutes

Cooking Time: 50 minutes

Servings: 6

Ingredients:

1 pound shredded imitation crab meat

½ cup mayonnaise

1 cup diced celery

¼ cup diced green onions

3 peeled and chopped hardboiled eggs

1 tablespoon lemon juice

Directions:

1. In a medium sized cup, put all the ingredients together with a lid.

2. Refrigerate to allow the flavors to blend for at least 1 hour before serving.

Olive Garden House Salad

The Olive Garden promotion of all-you-can-eat soup, salad, and breadsticks is one of the most successful marketing campaigns of all time. It has been duplicated in many other restaurant chains, such as the Endless Lunch from T.G.I. Friday and the Bottomless Express Lunch from Chili. Be rest assured this classic Italian salad will be a hit with friends and family. To make a true home Olive Garden meal, serve it with some breadsticks and soups.

Preparation Time: 5 minutes

Cooking Time: 50 minutes

Servings: 6

Ingredients:

1 bag of American Blend salad mix

10 black olives

10 slices red onion

8 banana peppers

1 sliced tomato

1 cup croutons

Olive Garden Salad Dressing, to taste

Directions:

1. In a medium container with lid, mix all of the ingredients.

2. Cool in the refrigerator for 1–2 hours with salad and serving dishes.

3. Put the dressing onto the plate bottom. Apply the ingredients of the chilled salad over the dressing.

Olive Garden Salad Dressing

It's quick to do the Olive Garden salad dressing at home, and tastes better than anything you would buy from the supermarket shelf. If placed in an airtight container in the refrigerator, the dressing can keep for around 10 days.

| Preparation | Time: | 5 | minutes |
| Cooking | Time: | 60 | minutes |

Servings: 6

Ingredients:

½ cup mayonnaise

1 teaspoon vegetable oil

1/3 cup white vinegar

2 tablespoons corn syrup

2 tablespoons Romano cheese

¼ teaspoon garlic salt

2 tablespoons Parmesan cheese

½ teaspoon Italian seasoning

1 tablespoon lemon juice Sugar (optional)

½ teaspoon parsley flakes

Directions:

1. Place all of the ingredients into a blender. Blend well until all is mixed.

2. If you consider the dressing a little tart to match your tastes, add some sugar.

Chapter 4: Pasta

Olive Garden's Fettuccine Alfredo

The dish is delicious and will please anyone's appetite.

Preparation Time: 5 minutes

Cooking Time: 25 minutes

Servings: 6

Ingredients:

½ cup butter, melted

2 tablespoons cream cheese

1 pint heavy cream 1 teaspoon garlic powder

Some salt

Some black pepper

⅔ cup parmesan cheese, grated

1 pound fettuccine, cooked

Directions:

Melt the cream cheese in the melted butter over medium heat until soft.

Add the heavy cream and season the mixture with garlic powder, salt, and pepper.

Reduce the heat to low and allow the mixture to simmer for another 15 to 20 minutes.

Remove the mixture from heat and add in the parmesan. Stir everything to melt the cheese.

Pour the sauce over the pasta and serve.

Spaghetti Pizza Recipe

This spaghetti pizza recipe is very easy to make, but it takes a little while. However, it really is worth it. It is a delicious and comforting dish and also has ground meat. Serve with a salad of green leaves and tomatoes, and some to toasted garlic bread. Let's go for the ingredient list and do it step by step!

Preparation Time: 5 minutes
Cooking Time: 30 minutes
Servings: 6

Ingredients:

750 ml of pasta sauce

500 g ground beef

500 g of spaghetti

400 g of tomatoes cut into small cubes

150 g sliced pepperoni

1 ½ cups shredded cheddar cheese

1 cup shredded Swiss cheese

½ cup grated Parmesan cheese

½ cup whole milk

1 chopped onion

3 cloves garlic, minced

2 chopped red or green peppers

1 teaspoon dried Italian seasoning

2 large eggs

Directions:

Gather the ingredients to make the spaghetti pizza.

Preheat the oven to 170 ° C. Boil a large pot of water to cook the spaghetti.

Cook the beef, chopped onion, chopped garlic and chopped red and green peppers in a pan over medium heat with oil until the meat is browned.

Drain well and add the pasta sauce, the tomatoes cut into small cubes and the Italian seasoning. Stir well and boil over medium heat while preparing spaghetti.

Cook the spaghetti according to the package instructions.

Combine the milk, eggs and grated Parmesan cheese in a large bowl and beat until mixed.

Strain the spaghetti and stir with the egg mixture. Spread half of the spaghetti, egg and milk mixture in a refractory dish and copper with half of the sauce and beef mixture. Repeat the layers.

Bake in a preheated oven for 30 or 40 minutes until hot, and cover with the remaining cheeses and then the pepperoni. Return to the oven and bake until the cheeses melt. Let stand for five minutes and cut into squares to serve the spaghetti pizza.

Garden Spaghetti Carbonara

This dish has the potential to become a new favorite.

Preparation Time: 5 minutes

Cooking Time: 50 minutes

Servings: 6

Ingredients:

1/4 cup of flour

1/4 cup butter

1 liter of milk

1/8 teaspoon of pepper

1/2 teaspoon of salt

18 oz bacon cut extra thick

1/4 cup of olive oil

12 oz sliced mushrooms

6 tablespoons of chopped shallots

Cook 1 pound spaghetti according to the package insert

2 teaspoons of finely chopped parsley

1/2 cup grated parmesan cheese

2 ounces of freshly grated Fontina cheese

Directions:

Melt butter over medium heat in a 4-quarter strong casserole dish. Remove the meal and cook for 1 minute. Add milk, salt, and pepper and stir vigorously with a whisk until barely boiling the mixture. Reduce heat and boil for 5 minutes while the sauce thickens. Stir in the Fontina cheese and allow it to melt in the sauce. Stay warm.

Thoroughly cook the bacon. Drain on paper towels. Cut into pieces of 1/4-inch and whisk in the sauce. In a large skillet, melt olive oil over medium heat. Add sliced onions and chopped mushrooms and sauté until golden; add to the sauce. Cook spaghetti according to the directions on the box. Drain well and add the parsley to the sauce. Mix well and pass to a serving table. Sprinkle with Parmesan cheese and serve as soon as possible.

Spaghetti Frittata

Frittatas are simply more resistant and easy to cook tortillas. They are one of the best quick recipes to prepare for brunch, breakfast, lunch or dinner. The only rules for making frittata are to make sure that the eggs are well-beaten and that the ingredients you add are well cooked before incorporating them. Only then can you succeed. You can use almost any leftover food such as rice, pasta, diced potatoes, cooked meat or vegetables. This time I will teach you how to make a spaghetti frittata step by step. Take note!

Preparation Time: 5 minutes
Cooking Time: 30 minutes
Servings: 6

Ingredients:

½ cup chopped green pepper or ½ cup chopped onion

2 tablespoons olive oil

1 tablespoon butter

¼ cup milk

2 cups grated Parmesan cheese

½ teaspoon dried basil leaves

1 cup cooked spaghetti or fettuccine cut into 5 cm pieces

6 eggs

Directions:

Heat the olive oil and butter in a pan until it melts.

Add the green pepper and cook over medium heat, stirring frequently until tender and crispy at the same time.

Meanwhile, in a large bowl, mix the eggs with the milk, ¼ cup grated Parmesan cheese, salt and pepper, and basil.

Add the cooked pasta to the egg mixture and stir gently.

Next, add the egg mixture to the pan and arrange the pasta in a uniform layer.

Cook the egg mixture over medium heat, raising the sides with a spatula occasionally so that the raw egg flows underneath.

When the egg mixture is almost ready, but still moist, after 10 minutes, cover it with grated Parmesan cheese. Cook for a few more minutes until it begins to brown. Remove from the oven and cut the frittata into pieces. Serve immediately.

Chapter 5: Chicken

Grilled Chicken Tenderloin

This hearty quick-and-easy breakfast wrap makes a perfect start to a great day.

Preparation Time: 10 min.

Marinating time 1 hour

Cooking time: 30 min.

Servings: 4–5

Ingredients:

4–5 boneless and skinless chicken breasts, cut into strips, or 12 chicken tenderloins, tendons removed

1 cup Italian dressing

2 teaspoons lime juice

4 teaspoons honey

Directions:

Combine the dressing, lime juice and honey in a plastic bag. Seal and shake to combine.

Place the chicken in the bag. Seal and shake again, then transfer to the refrigerator for at least 1 hour. The longer it marinates, the more the flavors will infuse into the chicken.

When ready to prepare, transfer the chicken and the marinade to a large nonstick skillet.

Bring to a boil, then reduce the heat and allow to simmer until the liquid has cooked down to a glaze.

Boston Market's Rotisserie Chicken Copycat

This simple 5-ingredient roast chicken is done in just five easy-to-follow steps, making a great family dinner during reunions and gatherings.

Preparation Time: 5 minutes

Cooking Time: 30 minutes

Servings: 6

Ingredients:

¼ cup apple cider vinegar

½ cup canola oil

2 tablespoons brown sugar

4 fresh garlic cloves, finely chopped

1 whole roasting chicken

Directions:

Combine vinegar, oil, sugar, and garlic in a bowl. Add chicken and spoon mixture on top to coat well. Refrigerate overnight, making sure to turn chicken over to soak opposite side

Remove chicken from refrigerator. Set aside for at least 20 minutes.

Bake at 350°F for about 45-50 minutes or until the temperature reads 165°F on an instant meat thermometer inserted in thickest part of the thigh without touching any bones.

Serve.

Apple Cheddar Chicken

Your whole family will love it and will ask you to make it more often.

Preparation Time: 5 minutes
Cooking Time: 30 minutes
Servings: 6

Ingredients:

5 cooked skinless chicken breasts, whole or cubed (Cracker Barrel uses the whole breast, but either option works just as well.)

2 cans apple pie filling

1 cup melted butter

1 row Ritz crackers, crushed

1 bag extra-sharp cheddar cheese

Directions:

Preheat the oven to 350°F.

Combine the chicken, apple pie filling, and cheddar cheese in a mixing bowl. Stir to combine.

Pour the mixture into a greased casserole dish.

Mix Ritz crackers with the melted butter. Spread over the casserole.

Bake for 45 minutes or until it starts to bubble.

Chapter 6: Beef and Pork

Panda Express' Beijing Beef

This sweet and spicy Panda Express replica is a perfect copy of the original. Satisfy your cravings in as quick as 45 minutes.

Preparation Time: 15 minutes
Cooking Time: 50 minutes

Serving: 4

Ingredients:

1 egg

¼ teaspoon salt

6 tablespoons water

9 tablespoons cornstarch

1 pound flank steak

4 tablespoons sugar

3 tablespoons ketchup

2 tablespoons vinegar

¼ teaspoon chili pepper, crushed

1 cup vegetable oil

1 teaspoon garlic, finely chopped

1 red bell pepper, chopped

1 green bell pepper, chopped

1 white onion, chopped

Directions:

To make the marinade, add egg, salt, 2 tablespoons water, and 1 tablespoon cornstarch in a bowl. Mix well.

Slice steak against the grain into small strips. Transfer into a Ziploc bag and pour marinade inside. Seal tightly. Shake bag gently to make sure the meat is well-coated. Set aside for at least 15 minutes.

To make the sauce, combine sugar, ketchup, vinegar, chili pepper, remaining 4 tablespoons water, and 2 teaspoons cornstarch in a bowl. Mix well. Cover and keep refrigerated.

Heat oil in a saucepan. Ready a bowl with 6 tablespoons cornstarch. Place beef in bowl and toss until fully coated. Shake off excess cornstarch and cook beef in hot oil until golden brown. Transfer onto a plate lined with paper towels.

Remove excess oil from saucepan. Toss in garlic, bell peppers, and onions and cook for about 2 minutes, stirring continuously. Transfer vegetables onto a plate.

In the same saucepan, add sauce and bring to a boil. Reduce heat to low and let simmer for 10 minutes.

Serve beef and vegetables with sauce poured on top.

Chipotle's Beef Barbacoa

Chipotle's Beef Barbacoa is perfect because they are tender and also delicious.

Preparation Time: 15 minutes
Cooking Time: 30 minutes

Serving: 4

Ingredients:

2 onions, diced

3 tablespoons olive oil

8 garlic cloves, minced

1 tablespoon taco seasoning

½ tablespoon oregano

1 7-ounce can of chipotle in adobo sauce

1 cup chicken broth

1 cup water

2 bay leaves

2 tablespoons apple cider vinegar

3 pounds beef roast

Directions:

Add all ingredients EXCEPT the beef in a blender or food processor.

Pulse until the spice mixture is well blended.

Add halt of the spice mixture to the bottom of a slow cooker.

Place beef in the slow cooker and top with the remaining spice mixture.

Slow cook for 8 hours on LOW or 4 hours on HIGH.

Remove the beef from cooker and shred.

If desired, for a saucier barbacoa beef, return shredded beef back to the slow cooker and mix with sauce. Cook for an additional 10-15 minutes on LOW.

Homemade Spicy Beef Jerky

Homemade Spicy Beef Jerky is one of the most consumed foods throughout the world.

Preparation Time: 15 minutes

Cooking Time: 30 minutes

Serving: 4

Ingredients:

1 kg of roulades from a butcher or another lean beef, 4-5mm thick slices

100 ml soy sauce

150 ml organic apple cider vinegar

1 tbsp Sambal Oelek *

Salt pepper

1 pinch of stevia *

Directions:

Mix the ingredients for the marinade thoroughly.

Remove any fat from the meat and cut it into the desired portions.

Put the meat and marinade alternately in a food bag.

If possible, squeeze the air out of the bag and seal it.

Leave to marinate in the fridge for twelve to 24 hours.

Drain, dab thoroughly with kitchen paper.

Allow drying on a grid at around 50 degrees in the oven (leave the air and a small gap open) or in the automatic dehydrator for about 8-10 hours.

Meatloaf

This is not too spicy and it tastes wonderful.

Preparation Time: 5 minutes

Cooking Time: 30 minutes

Servings: 6

Ingredients:

500 g of ground beef (lean)

1 whole egg

1 tablespoon cornmeal

3 large garlic cloves

1/2 medium onion

Salt to taste

100 g of sliced mozzarella

100 g sliced ham

1 large tomato sliced (without salt)

6 bacon slices (optional)

Directions:

Pass the garlic and onion through the processor, or mash well (so as not to burst the meat).

Season meat to taste.

Remove the cornmeal and eggs and mix well.

Soak a towel in a clean bowl, and wring well.

Place the cloth on a smooth surface, and put the meat on top.

Using the palm, spread the meat until it is about 1 cm thick.

In this order put the cheese, ham, and tomato layered in the dough (leaving a small gap at the edges for ease when rolling).

Roll like roll, close tightly with the aid of the cloth where the meat is, particularly at length so that the cheese does not escape while baking.

Place the bacon slices on the meat in a slightly greased way, or graze the meat surface with oil slightly.

Cook until well browned in a preheated oven at 280 ° C (high oven)

Chapter 7: Fish and Seafood

Tilapia Florentine

A traditional Florentine dish is meat or fish that is served on top of a spinach surface. We decided to make it more enjoyable.

Preparation Time: 15 minutes
Cooking Time: 30 minutes

Serving: 4

Ingredients:

One package (6 ounces) fresh baby spinach

Six teaspoons canola oil, divided

Four tilapia fillets (4 ounces each)

One egg, lightly beaten

2 tablespoons lime juice

Two teaspoons garlic-herb seasoning blend

1/4 cup grated Parmesan cheese

1/2 cup part-skim ricotta cheese

Directions:

Cook the spinach in 4 teaspoons of oil until wilted in a large nonstick skillet; drain. In the meantime, put tilapia in a fattened 13-in. x in 9. Baking platter. Drizzle with remaining lime juice and oil. Sprinkle with a blend to season.

Combine the egg, ricotta cheese and spinach in a small bowl; spoon filets over. Sprinkle with a cheese made with Parmesan.

Bake for 15-20 minutes at 375 °, or quickly with a fork until the fish flakes.

Cajun Jambalaya Pasta

You will flip when you get your taste of this jambalaya pasta.

Preparation Time: 10 minutes

Cooking Time: 50 minutes

Servings: 6

Ingredients:

¼ cup unsalted butter

¼ cup extra-virgin olive oil

1 pound andouille sausage or smoked sausage, sliced

1 pound boneless skinless chicken breast, cubed

1 bell pepper, diced

1 white onion, diced

3 stalks celery, diced

4 cloves garlic, minced

1 pound jumbo shrimp, peeled and deveined

2 cups red salsa

1 (6 -ounce) can hot tomato sauce

1 quart low-sodium chicken broth

1 bay leaf

¼ cup Italian parsley, chopped

½ bunch green onions

1 pound linguine pasta, cooked according to the package directions

Spice Blend

1 tablespoon creole seasoning

1 tablespoon garlic powder

1 tablespoon onion powder

2 teaspoons black pepper

1 teaspoon paprika

Pinch cayenne pepper

Garlic bread, for serving

Directions:

In a small dish, mix together all the spices for the spice blend.

Season the chicken chunks with 1 tablespoon of the spice blend. Mix until the chicken is well coated, and set it aside.

In a large saucepan, melt the butter and heat olive oil over medium heat.

When it is hot, add the sausage slices and cook for 5 minutes. Add the chicken and cook for about 10 minutes.

Next, add the bell pepper, onion, and celery. Mix in half of the remaining spice blend. Cook for approximately 10 minutes, then add the garlic and cook 1 more minute.

With 1 tablespoon of seasoning blend, season the shrimp and set it aside. Then add the rest of the spices to the saucepan and stir to combine.

Add the salsa, tomato sauce, chicken broth, and the bay leaf. Mix together and bring it to a boil, stirring it together so that everything is well combined. Don't forget to scrape the bottom of the pan for brown bits.

Reduce the heat and let it simmer, covered, for about 30 minutes. Once the 30 minutes is up, discard the bay leaf. Add the shrimp, parsley, and green onions, and cook, still covered for about 10 minutes more.

Serve over pasta with a slice of toasted garlic bread.

Avocado and Fish cake

Here is a great and light dish that you can enjoy whenever you are looking for a healthy and nutritious meal to enjoy. It is packed full of nutrients that you will fall in love with.

Preparation Time: 15 minutes
Cooking Time: 50 minutes

Serving: 4

Ingredients:

Round puff pastry

3 avocados

125g smoked salmon

100ml evaporated milk

Juice of half a lemon

Get fat

Garlic powder

Fresh coriander

Salt and ground black pepper

Directions:

Preheat the oven to 200 ° C.

Spread the puff pastry sheet on a tray greased with oil or butter and paint it with a beaten egg.

Place a sheet of aluminum foil over it and on this chickpeas or beans and bake for 12 minutes or until golden brown. Let it cool.

Peel two avocados and remove the stone with a knife. Remove the pulp with the help of a spoon and place it in a bowl with the evaporated milk and lemon juice.

Mix until a homogeneous preparation.

Add salt, garlic powder, and ground black pepper.

Spread the avocado cream over the puff pastry, once cold.

Peel the remaining avocado and remove the corozo. Cut it into thin strips and put them around the cake.

Crumble the smoked salmon and put it in the center.

Finally, decorate the avocado and fish pie with fat salt and coriander leaves.

Chapter 8: Vegetarian

Hollywood Bowl

It's a dish you should really try as soon as possible!

Preparation Time: 30 minutes

Cooking Time: 60 minutes

Servings: 8

Ingredients:

1 cup brown rice

½ cup green onions, finely chopped, light green and white parts only

1 zucchini, finely chopped

2 tomatoes, finely chopped

1 cucumber, finely chopped

3 to 4 tablespoons lemon juice, freshly squeezed

1 cup fresh cilantro leaves, chopped

¼ teaspoon freshly ground black pepper

Sea salt to taste

Directions:

Rinse the rice & place it in a saucepan with approximately 2 cups of water. Bring it to a boil over high heat. Once done; decrease the heat to low; cover & let simmer for 40 to 45 minutes, until the rice is tender.

Remove the pan from heat & let stand for 10 to 15 more minutes, covered.

Transfer the rice to a large-sized bowl & let cool until no longer steaming, for a couple of minutes.

Add the cucumber, zucchini, green onions, tomatoes, cilantro, 3 tablespoons lemon juice, salt & pepper; mix well. Taste & feel free to add more of lemon juice, if required.

To allow the flavors to meld; cover & let chill for 30 minutes.

Taste & adjust the amount of seasoning. Serve cold & enjoy.

Roasted Garlic Mashed Potatoes

It's a dinner you should really try as soon as possible!

Preparation Time: 10 minutes

Cooking Time: 40 minutes

Servings: 4 persons

Ingredients:

2 pounds Yukon Gold potatoes; quartered

½ cup parmesan cheese, grated

6 roasted garlic cloves, pressed

1 teaspoon freshly ground black or white pepper

3 sticks unsalted butter, at room temperature

1 ½ cups half and half, or to taste

2 teaspoons kosher salt

Directions:

Place the quartered potatoes in a large saucepan & cover with the salted cold water. Bring it to a boil over high heat. Once done; cover & decrease the heat to a simmer. Cook for 12 to 15 minutes, until tender. Drain well & place the potato cubes in a ricer; pressing to remove the skins.

Now, over low heat in the same saucepan; add the pressed garlic together with cheese, half and half, butter, pepper and salt. Fold the ingredients into the potatoes until mixed well. Taste & adjust the amount of seasonings, if required. Remove from the heat & serve hot.

Pumpkin Cream with Edible Mushrooms

You will absolutely go crazy when you get your first bite.

Preparation Time: 15 minutes
Cooking Time: 30 minutes

Serving: 4

Ingredients:

1 large pumpkin

500c.c. chicken broth

350g edible mushrooms

100g grated Parmesan cheese

1 onion

2 cloves of garlic

A splash of liquid cream

Salt and nutmeg c / n

Olive oil c / n

Directions:

Clean the pumpkin and peel it.

Cut it in half and pass a peeled garlic clove so that the pulp is impregnated with the flavor.

Place on a tray; pour a little olive oil over the pumpkin and bake for 60 minutes at 250 ° C.

After this period, place the baked pumpkin in a saucepan with the chicken stock and the peeled onion; cook for 20 minutes.

When the squash is soft, crush everything in a blender.

Add some grated Parmesan cheese and continue crushing.

Place some olive oil with the remaining garlic clove peeled and chopped and sauté the rolled edible mushrooms. When the mushrooms are cooked, reserve them.

Serve the pumpkin cream in soup dishes or clay casseroles with a little grated Parmesan cheese, salt and nutmeg, cream and mushrooms.

Chapter 9: Bread and Soups

Olive Garden Minestrone Soup

This classic Italian vegetable and pasta soup is set to become a family's favorite. Just like a dish at Olive Garden, serve with grilled cheese or a salad and bread sticks.

Preparation Time: 15 minutes

Cooking Time: 30 minutes

Serving: 4

Ingredients:

¼ cup minced celery

3 tablespoons olive oil

4 cloves minced garlic

½ cup frozen Italian-style green beans

1 small minced onion

½ cup chopped zucchini

2 (15-ounce) cans drained red kidney beans

4 cups vegetable broth

2 (15-ounce) cans drained small white bean

1 (14-ounce) can diced tomatoes, drained

½ cup shredded carrots

3 cups hot water

1½ teaspoons dried oregano

2 tablespoons minced fresh parsley

1½ teaspoons salt

½ teaspoon dried basil

½ teaspoon pepper

4 cups fresh baby spinach

¼ teaspoon dried thyme

½ cup small shell pasta

Directions:

1. Heat up the olive oil in a big soup pot over low heat.

2. For 5 minutes, sauté in the celery, garlic, onion, green beans and zucchini.

3. Add the broth, beans, carrots, washed tomatoes, boiling water and spices.

4. Allow the soup to a boil. Lower heat for 20 minutes, and simmer.

5. Add the pasta and spinach leaves. Cook for another 20 minutes.

Chicken Mushroom Soup

In some of the more sophisticated recipes, it is made with just wine. However, my version of a wassail is made with blood orange instead of cider. But it doesn't mean that it is any less festive.

Preparation Time: 10 minutes

Cooking Time: 4 hours and 10 minutes

Servings: 4

Ingredients:

½ cup All-purpose flour

5 boneless & skinless chicken breasts, cubed

½ small onion, diced

3 cups mushrooms, sliced

¼ cup carrots, diced

6 cups chicken Broth

¼ cup softened butter, at room temperature

3 cups heavy cream

½ teaspoon white pepper

1 teaspoon lemon juice, freshly squeezed

¼ teaspoon dried thyme

Ground black pepper & kosher salt, to taste

⅛ teaspoon dried tarragon

Directions:

Over medium heat in a large pot; heat the butter until completely melted and then toss in the onion, chicken, mushrooms & carrots. Sauté until the chicken is cooked through; cover the ingredients with the all-purpose flour.

Pour in the chicken broth, white pepper, thyme, tarragon, pepper & salt. Bring the mixture to a simmer & cook for 10 to 12 minutes.

Add the lemon juice and heavy cream. Let simmer again for 10 to 12 more minutes.

Serve hot & enjoy.

Honey Brown Bread

It is an exotic style bread! It's also very easy to make!

Preparation time: 30 minutes

Cooking time 30 minutes | Rising time 3–4 hours

Servings: 4

Ingredients:

1 ½ cups warm water (105ºF)

1 tablespoon sugar

2 ¼ teaspoons instant dry yeast (1 package)

2 cups bread flour

1 ¾ cups whole wheat flour

1 tablespoon cocoa powder

2 teaspoons espresso powder (or instant coffee)

1 teaspoon salt

2 tablespoons butter, softened

¼ cup honey

2 tablespoons molasses

Caramel coloring, or dark brown food coloring (optional)

¼ cup cornmeal, for dusting the bottom of the shaped (not baked) loafs (optional) Oats, for dusting the top of the shaped (not baked) loafs (optional)

Directions:

Mix together the warm water, sugar, and yeast, and set aside for five minutes.

If you have a stand mixer, it is easiest to use that or a bread machine to mix your dough. With the whisk attachment on the stand mixer, mix together the flours, cocoa powder, espresso powder (or finely ground instant coffee), and the salt.

Add the yeast mixture you set aside as well as the butter, honey, and molasses. You can also add the food coloring if you choose to use it. At this point, you will need to switch to your dough hook attachment and let the mixer run on a medium speed until a dough is formed. This may take as long as 10 minutes.

Lightly oil a large bowl and transfer the dough to the bowl. Cover with a towel and place in a warm spot for two hours. It should double in size.

After it has doubled, divide the dough into 6 pieces and form them into loaves. Place the cornmeal in a shallow dish and place each loaf in the cornmeal and then move to a lined baking sheet. Make sure you leave enough room between the loaves for them to expand. Sprinkle the loaves with some oats if you would like. Then spray a little bit of cooking spray on each loaf before covering them loosely with plastic wrap and then allow them to rise again for about an hour or an hour and a half.

Preheat the oven to 350°F.

After the loaves have doubled in size, remove the plastic wrap and transfer the pan to the oven.

Bake 25–35 minutes, then remove from the oven and let sit for about 10–15 minutes before slicing and serving.

Lemon Bread (Starbucks)

This makes for the perfect lunch to serve up whenever you want to truly spoil yourself.

Preparation time: 1 hour 10 minutes

Cooking time: 55 minutes

Servings: 15

Ingredients:

1/2 cup + 2 tbsp coconut flour

2/3 cup monkfruit classic

9 tbsp butter, melted

2 tbsp heavy whipping cream

2 tbsp cream cheese, softened

4 tsp fresh lemon juice

1 1/2 tsp baking powder

1 tsp vanilla

1/2 tsp salt

6 eggs

2 lemons, zested

For the glaze:

2 tbsp monkfruit powdered

1   tsp   lemon   zest

2 tsp fresh lemon juice

Splash of heavy whipping cream

Directions:

Melt the butter in the microwave and let it cool down.

In a mixing bowl, beat the eggs. Add in the salt, heavy whipping cream, baking powder, monkfruit classic, vanilla, and cream cheese. Mix thoroughly.

Add into the mixture the coconut flour, melted butter, lemon juice, and lemon zest. Mix thoroughly.

Transfer the mixture into a bread pan lined with paper parchment.

Preheat the oven to 325 degrees F.

Bake the bread batter for 55 minutes or until the top is starting to turn brown. To know that the bread is cooked thoroughly, insert a toothpick in the center and nothing sticks to the toothpick when you pull it out.

To make the glaze:

Whisk together the ingredients for the glaze until the texture is smooth.

Put the glaze on the bread while it is still warm. Spread the glaze and let it drip over the sides of the bread.

Chapter 10: Desserts

Pumpkin Custard with Gingersnaps

You will love this recipe and it will remind you of meals your grandma used to make.

Preparation Time: 15 minutes
Cooking Time: 30 minutes

Serving: 4

Ingredients:

Custard

8 egg yolks

1¾ cups (1 15-ounce can) pure pumpkin puree

1¾ cups heavy whipping cream

½ cup sugar

1½ teaspoons pumpkin pie spice

1 teaspoon vanilla

Topping:

1 cup crushed gingersnap cookies

1 tablespoon melted butter

Whipped Cream

1 cup heavy whipping cream

1 tablespoon superfine sugar (or regular sugar if you have no caster sugar)

½ teaspoon pumpkin pie spice

Garnish

8 whole gingersnap cookies

Directions:

Preheat the oven to 350°F.

Separate the yolks from 8 eggs and whisk them together in a large mixing bowl until they are well blended and creamy.

Add the pumpkin, sugar, vanilla, heavy cream and pumpkin pie spice and whisk to combine.

Cook the custard mixture in a double boiler, stirring until it has thickened enough that it coats a spoon.

Pour the mixture into individual custard cups or an 8×8-inch baking pan and bake for about 20 minutes if using individual cups or 30–35 minutes for the baking pan, until it is set, and a knife inserted comes out clean.

While the custard is baking, make the topping by combining the crushed gingersnaps and melted butter. After the custard has been in the oven for 15 minutes, sprinkle the gingersnap mixture over the top.

When the custard has passed the clean knife test, remove from the oven and let cool to room temperature.

Whisk the heavy cream and pumpkin pie spice together with the caster sugar and beat just until it thickens.

Serve the custard with the whipped cream and garnish each serving with a gingersnap.

BJ's Peanut Butter S'mores Pizookie

This dish will certainly please your sweet tooth.

Preparation Time: 20 minutes

Cooking Time: 20 minutes

Servings: 8

Ingredients:

⅓ cup light brown sugar, lightly packed

1 stick unsalted butter, melted

½ teaspoon vanilla

1 large egg plus 1 egg yolk

⅓ cup granulated sugar

1 ¼ cups all-purpose flour

2 Graham crackers, broken into large pieces

½ teaspoon baking soda

1 Hershey's bar, broken into large pieces

¾ cup semisweet chocolate chips

4 marshmallows, cut in half

½ teaspoon salt

Directions:

Preheat your oven to 400 F. Spray 2 cast iron baking dishes or pie plates, 6" each with the nonstick cooking spray.

Stir the butter with granulated sugar & brown sugar using a rubber spatula in a large bowl until combined well. Let stand for a couple of minutes. Stir in the vanilla and egg. Add the baking soda, flour & salt; continue to stir the ingredients until incorporated well. Fold in the chocolate chips.

Evenly divide the dough into 4 pieces. Press two pieces of dough into the bottom of the prepared pans.

Divide the Hershey's bar, graham cracker & marshmallows between the dough. Flatten out the leftover two pieces of dough; pressing on top of the marshmallows.

Bake in the preheated oven until edges are slightly browned but the inside is still gooey, for 12 to 15 minutes. Let cool for a couple of minutes then serve.

Starbucks' Iced Lemon Pound Cake

Your whole family will love it and will ask you to make it more often.

Preparation Time: 20 minutes

Cooking Time: 20 minutes

Servings: 8

Ingredients:

Loaf

1½ cups all-purpose flour

2 teaspoons baking powder

½ teaspoon salt

3 large eggs

1 cup granulated sugar

1 cup sour cream

½ cup vegetable oil

2 tablespoons lemon zest

1 tablespoon lemon extract, or to taste

Lemon Glaze

1 cup powdered sugar

3 tablespoons lemon juice

Directions:

Preheat oven to 350°F. Grease and flour a loaf pan.

In a bowl, combine flour, baking powder and salt. Set aside.

In a mixer bowl, beat the eggs, sugar, and sour cream until well-blended.

Continue beating while adding oil in a stream.

Add lemon zest and extract and mix.

Add the flour mixture and mix just to incorporate. The batter will be lumpy.

Pour batter into prepared loaf pan and spread evenly with a spatula.

Bake for 40 minutes and then tent with foil.

Let bake until toothpick inserted at the center comes out with just a few crumbs (about 10–12 minutes).

Place pan on a wire rack for loaf to cool completely.

Meanwhile, prepare the glaze. Whisk powdered sugar while adding lemon juice gradually until the right consistency is achieved.

Remove loaf from pan and drizzle with glaze.

Conclusion

Copycat restaurant dishes have actually become preferred with the ever-high price of dining in restaurants. This book has actually shown to you secret dishes from all your preferred restaurants in America so you can prepare them in the convenience of your residence.

Hanging out with family and friends at dining establishments has actually come to be a trend nowadays. It may be the delicious and also remarkable preference of their recipes. It might be that we just wish to interact socially. Whatever the factor is, consuming homemade food has its relevance. You'll have the ability to manage your food sections as well as preserve a well balanced diet regimen. It will certainly aid you save both money and time, together with establishing a healthier food pattern. If you have actually constantly wished to cook your favored restaurant recipes in your home without investing a fortune, it's currently feasible.

Via making these dishes on your own rather than eating out, you'll simply see just how much you actually saved for each recipe and also you'll recognize what I am discussing. Remember, do not limit on your own and also experiment, be innovative and have fun!

You could find yourself in the circumstance of not being able or going to most likely to your preferred dining establishment to appreciate several of the tasty dishes they serve there. You may lack transport, have a clinical problem, or just not like having dishes in public rooms, in addition to that maybe you are aiming to conserve some cash or time. You are probably looking to either order takeout food or prepare those very same tasty dishes by yourself. Cooking them on your own is the better option because it's less costly as well as really not too lengthy.

If you find yourself in this group, then this book is committed to you, although anyone thinking about finding out the secrets behind these restaurant-famous recipes rates to review. Envision exactly how wonderful it will certainly be to be responsible for the top quality of the food you eat, exactly how amazed your liked ones will certainly be, as well as just how much money you will certainly save by choosing to cook your own food at home. You have the option to do your regular buying, buy all the active ingredients you require, as well as prepare the meals you love at your own rate and in the convenience of your own residence.

It just takes a little bit of creative thinking, interest, and ingenuity to become a better cook, as there are thousands of recipes worldwide that will make you salivate. I such as to assume that this publication is the ideal push forward to make you love home-cooked meals as well as to become addicted to by doing this of life.

If you are a food-driven heart, having an actually great meal is among the wonderful satisfaction of life. Such a benefit might be also better taking into consideration the labor of eating in restaurants-- making a reservation, getting ready as well as, of course, calming down to order. But the most magical minute of all is when the long-awaited food shows up-- moving with a crowed dining-room as well as prepared to be delighted in prior to being put on the table. Consisting of beautifully created salads and incredibly well crunchy, scrumptious fried all points to silky spaghetti as well as flawlessly cooked steaks-- great food for the dining establishments always seems to have a little extra to make it show.

Hanging out with family and friends is essential for the good of all. It can prevent isolation related to depression, heart disease, as well as unsafe health problems. With a little effort, cooking can assist you come to be more social. Have your kids go to the kitchen area with you - give them straightforward tasks when they are young - or cook with close friends. If you want to make brand-new buddies, consider cooking courses where you can communicate with classmates as you learn brand-new skills. And do not neglect the social benefits that you obtain when your dish prepares. Lots of women more than happy to be able to supply homemade food to friends and family at numerous events. Food is usually consulted with a smiling face and also a wish to return the support.

The biggest advantage of using copycat restaurant dishes is that not just can you conserve money, but, if required, you can tailor the dishes. For instance, if you wish to lower the salt or butter in one of the plates, you can. Now you have actually saved money, and at the same time supplied a nutritious meal for your household.

You have little control over the active ingredients in the meal when you dine in restaurants. You can't, certainly, change the recipe that you order due to the fact that sauces, and so on are made in advance.

It is not actually that hard to learn exactly how to prepare supersecret dining establishment dishes. Some assume you require a degree in culinary arts or cooking education and learning so you can prepare those secret recipes. Any person can collect the components themselves as well as cook an expensive dish that tastes like the real point.

Cooking supersecret recipes from dining establishments will certainly likewise make your friends and family ask yourself where you have actually found out to cook so well. Imagine cooking an entire meal that appears like it was the restaurant's take-out food. I wager some friends of yours won't also think you've cooked it!

CPSIA information can be obtained
at www.ICGtesting.com
Printed in the USA
BVHW010939210421
605287BV00012B/255